WONDERFUL WEIRD ANIMALS

Contents

Susan Ring

Sometimes Bigger Is Better

Bigger feet can help an animal balance or keep from sinking. This bird's big, long toes may look strange. But they keep the bird from sinking into the water. The bird spreads out its toes to walk across lily pads.

NAME: Jacana

WHERE IT LIVES: Tropical and subtropical lakes and ponds

FACT: These birds build nests on plants that float on the water.

Big, big ears can help an animal hear better. When they hunt at night, these foxes use their big ears to find food and avoid enemies.

NAME: Bat-eared Fox

WHERE IT LIVES: Dry places in Africa

FACT: These foxes are mainly insectivores, which means they eat insects.

Looking bigger, even for a little while, can help an animal scare away enemies.

When this lizard sees danger coming, it opens the ruffle around its neck. Enemies think the lizard is larger than it is.

NAME: Australian Frilled Lizard

WHERE IT LIVES: Dry forests and woodlands of Australia and New Guinea

FACT: When the lizard is no longer alarmed, its ruffle folds down and its mouth closes.

Protective Coverings

NAME: Io Moth

WHERE IT LIVES: Eastern North America

FACT: The markings on its lower wings are called eyespots.

Some animals have markings that make them look like something else. When enemies see the spots on this moth's wings, they turn away. The spots look like the eyes of a big, hungry animal.

This crab hides by piling seaweed and sponges on its shell. When hungry fish swim by, they see the seaweed and sponges. But they do not see the crab underneath!

NAME: Decorator Crab

WHERE IT LIVES:
Tropical seas

FACT: When it moves to a new spot, the crab changes its decorations.

A pangolin looks like it's covered with armor. When it is afraid, it rolls itself up into a ball. Other animals can't scratch the pangolin's tough scales.

When the pangolin goes hunting for insects, its scaly skin protects it from bug bites.

Weird but Wonderful

When scientists first saw this animal, they did not believe that it could be real. A platypus is like a duck in some ways. It has a bill and webbed feet.

It is like a beaver in other ways. It has brown fur and a flat tail.

Its webbed feet and flat tail help the platypus swim. It uses its bill to scoop up food in the water.

When it is on land, it uses its claws to dig and grab.

NAME: Hammerhead Shark

WHERE IT LIVES: Tropical and subtropical waters around the world

FACT: This shark has one eye and one nostril on each end of its flat, wide head.

How might its wonderfully weird head help this shark hunt in the sea?